Pages and pages of swashbuckling, crazy pirates to colour! Get this handy, bag-shaped colouring book for your little one. This easy-to-carry book with cute, black-and-white illustrations to colour is the perfect companion for every preschooler.

- Will keep children occupied for hours
- Fun way for children to learn about colours and colouring
- Ideal book to improve children's motor skills and encourage creativity

COLOURMANIA

Scan Now!

Children | Colouring
US$ 4.95

978-81-319-3744-0

PEGASUS
www.pegasusforkids.com
₹90

9 788131 937440
001